D0613822

BRIA

ie,

nsion
o

s the

r

Victorian and Edwardian

NORTHUMBRIA

from old photographs

Introduction and commentaries by

J. W. THOMPSON *and* D. BOND

B. T. BATSFORD LTD
LONDON

First published 1976
Reprinted 1981, 1984

Text © J. W. Thompson & D. Bond 1976

ISBN 0 7134 3092 3

Printed and bound in Great Britain by
Anchor Brendon Ltd, Tiptree, Essex
for the publishers B. T. Batsford Ltd
of 4 Fitzhardinge Street, London W1A 0AH

CONTENTS

3 Sandhill, 1894: At the time the photograph was taken, Sandhill was devoted almost entirely to the purposes of trade and commerce. The five-storey house, five bays wide, to the left of the centre of the photograph belonged to Aubone Surtees, a Newcastle banker. In November 1772, Bessie, his daughter, with the help of a ladder, eloped with John Scott to Scotland where they were married the next day. John Scott later rose to the position of Lord High Chancellor of England, and became Baron Eldon of Eldon

ACKNOWLEDGEMENTS

The authors and publishers would like to thank the following for permission to reproduce the photographs in this book: Birmingham Public Library nos 1, 117, 147; Major A. S. C. Browne nos 98a, 98b; Durham County Libraries (Darlington District Library) nos 13, 79, 82, 132; Mrs Hirst no. 21; Lord Londonderry nos 43, 114, 146; Mr S. Martin nos 33, 34, 149; Newcastle Public Library nos 108, 119; Newcastle Public Library (Auty-Hastings Collection) nos 3–12, 14–20, 22–32, 35, 37–39, 44–46, 49–62, 64, 65, 67–76, 80, 81, 83–85, 87–91, 97, 99–107, 109, 110a, 110b, 111, 112, 115, 116, 120–131, 133a, 133b, 134, 137, 138, 140, 142, 145, 148; Newcastle Public Library (Lowrey Collection) nos 2, 31a, 66, 77, 86, 92–96, 113, 118, 135, 136; Northumberland County Record Office nos 40–42, 48, 78, 89, 139, 141, 143, 144; Miss Rutherford no. 47; Mr Sullivan no. 63. No. 36 is from the publishers' collection.

The authors also wish to mention the following people, because without their help and guidance the book would not have been possible: Mr Gordon Clarke, for producing such marvellous copies from the original plates and photographs; Miss Pat Twentyman for transcribing our rough notes into neat typewritten copy; Mr Noel Hanson for his expert advice on trams and trains and all our many friends who have given us advice on various other subjects; Dr N. McCord of Newcastle University for reading and correcting our final script; and last but not least the City Librarian, Newcastle City Libraries, for his co-operation.

INTRODUCTION

4 Sunderland: Fawcett Street. On the left is the Town Hall, built in 1890 by J. and T. Tillman, who were Sunderland architects. *c.*1903–04

Northumbria was once a kingdom of the British Isles stretching from the Humber to the Firth of Forth; a kingdom which, in the 7th century, was the most powerful in the country, and one which was the centre of culture, learning and literature. Gradually, however, the kingdom became less powerful, it was broken up and the lands were renamed. It is not until we reach the twentieth century that the name Northumbria, once more, comes into general use. It is a name used to promote "an area of outstanding natural beauty" to tourists – "Northumbria, a holiday kingdom." This Northumbria, however, refers to a much smaller area than its ancient counterpart. It is a convenient "umbrella" under which to group the pre-April 1974 areas of Northumberland, Durham and Newcastle. In Victorian and Edwardian times and even to the present day these three names to the rest of the world would be synonymous with coal, pit heaps and the dirt that went with them. In actual fact this North-East corner of England had and does have vast open tracts of land: some wild moorland, some used for sheep and cattle and some cultivated for crops. The industrial area then lay principally round its rivers.

The nineteenth-century Industrial Revolution did not bring vast changes to the North East; it merely increased the pace of industrialisation. The need was to get the area's coal to the other rapidly expanding industrial areas as fast as possible. As the demand grew, therefore, mines began to spring up further away from the riversides. Quicker methods had to be found to transport it. At first wooden wagonways with horse-drawn trucks were used to haul the coal to the staithes on the rivers. Then followed other mechanical inventions for hauling the coal and finally came the steam locomotive. Following on from this in 1825 came the world's first public railway system, the Stockton-Darlington Railway. This revolutionary invention spread rapidly so that when Queen Victoria came to the throne in 1837 railways were beginning to be part of the English way of life, transporting not only people but goods including, of course, coal.

With the growth of railways there came an increased demand for iron to build them. This too was found in the North-East area at Cleveland in North Yorkshire. Gradually, with the increase in different types of industry different types of coal were needed, so it was found for example that good coking coal came from Durham and steam coal from Northumberland.

By the mid-nineteenth century, however, the Midland coalfields could get their coal to the Capital quicker than the coal from the North East. Sir Charles Mark Palmer took up this challenge and in 1852 launched the first screw-propelled iron collier, the *John Bowes*. It was indeed a "juggernaut" of its day, capable of carrying 650 tons of coal to London and returning in five days instead of a month.

From iron-built colliers it was not long before iron warships were being built. The first was again from Palmer's yard at Jarrow and it was called *The Terror*. It was launched in 1854 for use in the Crimean War. The Crimean War also played an important part in the rise of another great industry on Tyneside. Sir William G. Armstrong had established a general engineering works on the riverside at Elswick. It was here in 1859 that he developed his Elswick Ordnance works and by 1882 he was constructing naval warships at the Elswick works where he was able to fit the guns and armour.

So Northumbria's great industrial age was established with coal, railways and ships.

There were many "firsts" for the area during this Victorian and Edwardian period which had a great bearing on the life in the area. Three were of particular note.

In 1878 Joseph W. Swan made the first successful incandescent lamp and the first public use of electricity was outside Swan's shop in Mosley Street, Newcastle. Sir William G. Armstrong's house at Rothbury, Northumberland, was the first house in the country to be lit by electricity.

In 1884, Charles A. Parsons patented the steam turbine so revolutionizing speed on water.

Finally, we should mention the building on the Tyne by Armstrong, Mitchell and Co of the first real oil tanker, the *Glückauf*. She was launched in 1885 and discharged her first cargo in July 1886 at Geestmunde, Germany, and her tanks proved to be "impervious to leakage".

Whilst the industrial area of the region was expanding and consolidating its position, what about the large towns? There were no "fashionable" towns like Bath or Cheltenham. Most of them had become commercial centres for the newly thriving industries. The buildings were not erected as show places, but had a utilitarian purpose. Newcastle is the one exception. It was a town which had still been medieval in character in the 1830s. It was crowded onto the banks of the Tyne, had narrow streets, half-timbered houses and for the most part kept within the confines of the City walls. Three men, however, had the courage to transform and re-develop the old City centre so it could fulfil its modern function as the great commercial capital of the region. They were Richard Grainger, builder, John Dobson, architect, and John Clayton, Town Clerk. So Newcastle had the unique position of being the only major city in England with a planned centre. It became a city of well-planned streets and high stone-faced buildings. One outstanding building was the great Newcastle Central Railway Station opened by Queen Victoria in 1850. There was the fine curve of Grey Street described by Sir John Betjeman as "one of the best streets in England". The fruit and vegetable markets were considered "the most spacious and magnificent in Europe".

The increase in industry brought great numbers of workers to the area. Newcastle's population rose from 70,504 in 1841 to 266,603 in 1911, Durham County's from 307,963 in 1841 to 1,369,667 in 1911 and Northumberland County's from 266,020 in 1841 to 697,335 in 1911. As the population grew so did the need for houses and so Newcastle's suburbs expanded. There was during this second half of the nineteenth century a spirit of change which had never before been so active in Newcastle. It could almost be likened to this second half of the twentieth century where the City's re-development is like a whole way of life being torn down and a new one rebuilt.

What of the rest of Northumberland and Durham, the rural and coastal areas? Northumberland, famous for its sheep, especially the black-faced Cheviot sheep, and Durham for its short-horn cattle. Fishing was once the North-East area's most important occupation. There were the ports like Hartlepool and North Shields, with their large fleets of herring drifters and steam trawlers, as well as numerous small fishing villages, especially in Northumberland, like Seahouses, Beadnell and Newbiggin with their fleets of cobles, fishing for lobsters and crabs. Also commercially important was the seasonal salmon fishing at places like Berwick.

Victorian and Edwardian Northumbrians were strong, hardworking, industrious people, but like other places in the country there were still present the "two nations" of the rich and the poor. The new wealthy industrialists were building their large houses on the outskirts of the towns and cities. The workers on the other hand were living, in many cases, in extremely crowded conditions because houses were not being built quickly enough to cope with the influx of labour into the industrial areas.

In the country a feudal system survived, with the "Squire" living in his castle or hall and his tenants farming his land. Here in the country, however, life was at a much slower pace, and there was fresh air, something the cities and towns lacked. So in 1845 recommendations were made for the provision of public parks. As the century progressed parks and recreational spaces were developed, often given by the great industrialists who realised that their workers needed fresh air and exercise if they were to be fit and healthy. Sir William G. Armstrong gave Armstrong Park and Jesmond Dene to Newcastle. Also at this time the seaside holiday became popular and places like Whitley Bay and Saltburn developed into popular resorts.

The Victorian period was the first camera age and it saw the rise of many professional photographers. It was the introduction of the wet collodion plate which heralded a general expansion of photography. Not, however, until the 1870s, with the introduction of the dry-plate process which finally freed the photographer from his studio, was he able to get out and about. Joseph W. Swan of Newcastle took out over 70 patents in connection with photography and it was in 1877 that he made his first dry gelatine bromide plates.

In preparing this work for publication we have examined some 20,000 glass plates and photographs. Our task of reducing this number, to those we have selected, was enormous. All were of great interest, but we used the following three criteria in our final choice:

1. Did the photograph show people working or enjoying themselves or just walking about?

2. Would the photograph be of interest locally, showing a bygone way of life and bring back memories?

3. Would the local scenes be of sufficient interest to show the rest of the country what life was like in the North-East area during this Victorian and Edwardian period?

We looked at many individual photographs and collections of glass plates, but we feel three of the collections must be specifically referred to: the Auty-Hastings and Lowrey Collections belonging to Newcastle City Libraries, and the Mitford Collection in the care of the Northumberland Record Office.

Matthew Auty was born in 1850 and served his apprenticeship as a tobacconist eventually establishing his own business in Tynemouth. It was during this period that his interest in photography developed and he used to take local views which he sold in his shop. He eventually became a member of the old Newcastle and Northern Counties Photographic Association. It was through his membership of this association, and his growing friendship with a Mr J. P. Gibson that Auty was encouraged to launch into photography. This he did at a double-fronted house in Front Street, Tynemouth. At the same time he was running a tobacco business in King Street, South Shields. Auty realised that landscape and view publication work was his strong point rather than portrait photography, so he employed Mr R. E. Ruddock for portraiture. This partnership was dissolved, however, about 1892 when Mr Ruddock set up on his own in Newcastle.

Mr Auty was a good salesman and he never experienced any difficulty in finding shop-keepers to sell his views. Those were the days before the picture postcard had come into use and so adversely affected the view publishing business, although at a later date Auty's well-known picture postcards were printed from his plates. Up to the end of 1894 Mr Auty used to go round personally and keep in touch with his customers, but heart trouble caused his early death, at the age of 45, in 1895.

His business carried on for a while under its own momentum, but eventually the publication side and collection of negatives were taken over by Mr Godfrey Hastings of Whitley Bay. In a printed Auty catalogue published in 1898 after Auty's death the following paragraph appears.

> In bringing this catalogue before the notice of their customers, both private and trade, Messrs Auty Ltd would point out that such a work must of Necessity be a complete list only for a short space of time, as new subjects are continually being added, while, on the other hand, views which for various reasons become ''out of date'' have to be replaced or removed altogether although in this case the old negatives are never intentionally destroyed as it often happens that some changes cause these old views to be of value.

These glass plates were eventually presented in 1941 to the Newcastle Society of Antiquaries by Miss Hastings, sister of Mr Godfrey Hastings. A note in the Proceedings of the Society of Antiquaries for 1943 states ''we hope to print shortly a note by Miss Hastings on her brother's share in forming the collection''. Regrettably this note does not appear ever to have been published. The plates lay in the Keep of the Castle and were stored under poor conditions, so about 1946 it was decided that they should be handed over to the Newcastle City Libraries in whose care they now are. The Lowrey Collection was acquired quite unexpectedly by the City Libraries in June 1974. It came to us after Mr Lowrey of Chapel House Estate, Newcastle upon Tyne saw a brief note that someone else had donated slides to the library. He wondered if the library would be interested in a thousand which he had in his possession! They had originally belonged to his friend, a Mr Bell who worked as a foreman joiner for Newcastle Corporation during the latter part of the nineteenth and the early part of the twentieth century. Mr Bell had been a keen amateur photographer and with his job as a foreman joiner for the Corporation he must have been aware of the new developments in the City, major events and occasions, and most of all he recorded everyday events, picnics, outings, etc., so these photographic plates now come to us as a social record of the period.

The last collection we would mention is the Mitford Collection housed at the Northumberland Record Office. Mitford is a village some 17 miles north-west of Newcastle. The Rev. R. C. MacLeod was Vicar there from 1896–1934. He moved to Mitford originally for his wife's health. He was a well-liked man and took a great interest in the people in his parish and their activities. He took photographs at many of their outings and functions. Then on winter evenings he would give lantern shows to his parishioners as well as travelling throughout the diocese. We considered therefore, that this was an important collection of rural photographs because they both contrasted and complemented the much more urban photographs in the Lowrey Collection.

DURHAM COUNTY

5 Darlington: the Town Hall. The photograph was taken (1897) looking up Tubwell Row towards High Row. The Town Hall itself and the attached covered market were designed by Alfred Waterhouse, later President of the RIBA, and erected in 1863. The clock tower was presented to the town by Edward Pease. This building continued to be the centre of civic affairs in Darlington until the new Town Hall was opened by HRH The Princess Anne in 1970. The Golden Cock Hotel on the right is an old coaching inn

CHURCH ST. BLAYDON. 1475. G.n.g.

CHURCH ST BLAYDON. 1475. G.n.g.

CHICHESTER CROSSING, SO SHIELDS. 5008. G.N/C

6 *Left* Blaydon: Church Street (1890). This street linked the Blaydon–Gateshead road (seen at the junction) with the Blaydon–Newcastle road. The Boot and Shoe warehouse of Alfred Tyler and Son can be seen on the left. The white-painted building on the right was later demolished and replaced by Laws Stores. The tower in the left background belongs to St Cuthbert's Church, the Parish Church. This was erected in 1844, and is a stone building in the Early English style

7 *Below left* South Shields: Chichester Crossing. The photograph was taken from the Dean Tram Depot approach road and shows the complicated track and overhead layout (*c.*1906)

8 *Below* Spennymoor: High Street. The main road between the City of Durham and Bishop Auckland, *c.*1894. Spennymoor experienced a rapid advance in importance, wealth and population owing to coal mining and the establishment of the Weardale Iron and Coal Company. The photograph was taken looking South

9 South Shields: King Street (*c*.1905). One of the main thoroughfares in the town showing in the distance the railway line and one of the horse-drawn trams which was mounted on an Eade's patent reversible truck. This service ceased in 1906 before the introduction of electric tramways

CHANNEL SQUADRON SUNDERLAND SEPT 1903 2926 CH WB

10 Sunderland: The Channel Squadron. The visit of the nine vessels of the Channel Fleet took place from Tuesday 15 September to Friday 18 September, 1903. The weather had been extremely stormy and it was thought the Fleet would just steam on to Leith. However, the storms abated and, despite a still heavy swell, people were able to go out in boats round the ships, some of the more hardy boarding the vessels

11 *Above* South Shields Beach. A very busy afternoon on the beach, about 1908 and judging by the parasols in evidence in the foreground, a very hot afternoon too

12 *Above right* Sunderland, *c.*1910. The Wearmouth Bridge is seen in the background. Passing over the bridge are some top-covered tramcars with open balconies. Six of these were supplied to Sunderland in 1906. The vessel in the foreground (*Boltonhall*) is a steel-screw schooner of 3,595 tons. The original Wearmouth Bridge was constructed between 1793 and 1796 and was a toll bridge until 1885, although tolls for pedestrians were abolished in 1846. This bridge was replaced by the present structure in 1929.

13 *Right* Darlington Red Cross. Darlington branch of the Red Cross opened their Voluntary Aid Detachment hospital in the Friends Meeting House in September 1914. The picture shows some of the nursing staff with wounded Belgian soldiers. The Meeting House was in Skinnergate, and normally accommodated nearly 1,000 people

14 *Below* Jarrow: Ormonde Street. The unmade state of the road would have altered very shortly after this photograph was taken, as the laying of the tramlines began early in 1906, two years after this picture was taken

15 *Right* Haswell: Front Street (*c.*1897) The building adjoining Robson's grocer's shop is a public house (the Masons' Arms). Note the gleaming steps in front of the doorways of the houses on the left side of the street

16 *Below right* Stockton: On the Tees (*c.*1905). A paddle steam ferry leaving the landing stage on the Stockton side. Note the shipyards on the Thornaby side

17 Thornaby, *c.*1905 This view
shows tram No 6 of the Imperial
Tramways Company in Mandale
Road. The conductor can just be
seen entering the lower saloon

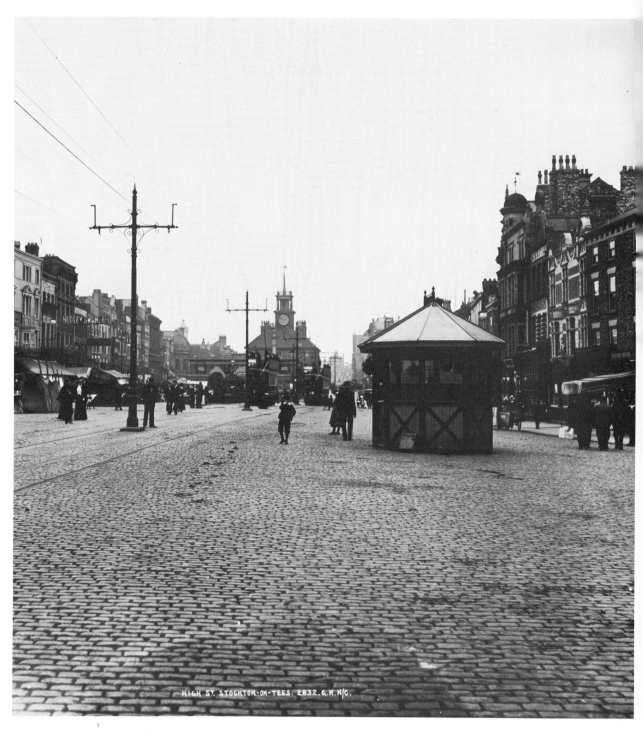

HIGH ST. STOCKTON-ON-TEES. 2832. G.H. N/C.

18 Stockton: High Street (*c*.1905), which was nearly half a mile in length and up to 180 feet in width. Trams Nos 1 and 19 of the Imperial Tramways Co are seen in the High Street. Both are double-bogied, open-topped trams running on 3' 6" track. Tram No 1 was the car used on the first official run when the new electric route was opened on 16 July 1898, linking Stockton and Middlesbrough

SHIPBUILDING

19 Newcastle. HMS *Superb*, an early Dreadnought battleship launched on 6 November 1907 at the Elswick works of Sir W. G. Armstrong, Whitworth & Co Ltd by Lady Anne Lambton

20 *Left* Shipyard workers leaving Wallsend slipway. The almost completed *Mauretania* can be seen in the background of the photograph (1907)

21 *Right* On the day of launch of the *Mauretania,* 20 September 1906, the funnels of the ship were placed end to end in the builders' yard to form a tunnel for the passage of motor cars containing parties of guests

22 *Below* The *Mauretania* finally leaves the Tyne for Liverpool on 22 October 1907

MOTOR CARS PASSING THROUGH THE FUNNEL CASINGS, OF R.M.S."MAURETANIA",
YARD OF THE ENGINE BUILDERS, THE WALLSEND SLIPWAY & ENGINEERING C?

23 Looking across the Tyne to the Elswick works of Sir W. G. Armstrong, Mitchell & Co Ltd. Elswick shipyard became famous for the battleships and warships built there

24 HMS *Victoria*, launched 9 April 1887, at the Elswick yard of Sir W. G. Armstrong, Mitchell & Co. The vessel was to have been called *Renown*, but was subsequently given the Queen's name in recognition of her Jubilee Year. She is seen here passing through the Swing Bridge, which was specially constructed by the Company to allow large ships to pass up and down the river. The wood paddle tug at the rear of the vessel was the *Sensation*

FISHING

25a and b *This page* North Shields. Two photographs (1896) of the Fish Quay, which was established in the early 1870s by Tynemouth Corporation, close to the Low Lighthouse

26a and b *Opposite page* Newbiggin-by-the-sea (c.1890) was a popular Victorian "watering place" and fishing village

27 *Above* Cullercoats: Brown's Buildings, in existence since 1836 and described by W. W. Tomlinson as "a fairly typical row of fishermen's cottages". The various types of baskets used by the fisher folk can be seen. The creels which the woman carried on their backs with the fish in, are on the left of the picture, and on the right, on top of an outhouse, can be seen a line swill

28 *Right* Fishing for salmon on the banks of the Tweed 1900. The method has remained unchanged for years. The net is loaded onto the stern of a small rowing boat. The boat sets off into the river in a circular route releasing the net as the boat travels round. The boat then comes back to its starting point and the net is winched in, gathering up the salmon into a bag.

ACKING HERRING
RTH SUNDERLAND. 5252. G.H.M/C.

29 *Above* Seahouses, *c.*1890:
packing herring for export to
Germany, Scandinavia, Russia,
etc. The girls, who were very
deft at packing the barrels,
followed the herring fleets
round the country

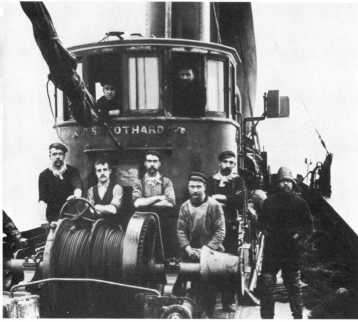

30 *Left* The *St Gothard*
photographed at sea near the
Farne Islands, *c.*1910. The boat
was probably a herring drifter
rigged for steam trawling and
was built by J. T. Eltringham &
Co at South Shields

31a and b Fish sorters on the Fish Quay, North Shields (c.1898) The two girls on the left (*above*) are wearing the fishwives' traditional flannel skirts with numerous tucks. The idea was that the more tucks there were in the skirt, the better was the style

32 Holy Island fisherwomen, *c*.1885: Sarah and Bessie Morris, who used to carry their fish to the mainland on the backs of their two mules and hawk it round the mainland villages

MINING

33 *Left* Pitmen, *c.*1900. The cage is arriving at the surface, bringing miners up at the end of a shift underground. The men are carrying their safety lamps.

34 *Above* Shaft sinkers waiting to descend into the pit, *c.*1900. The sinkers' job was, in fact, to construct the pit by either boring, digging or drilling. Hand drilling was in use as late as 1898. In sinking, a shift was of only 4 hours duration, followed by an 8 hour break, and then another 4 hour shift

35 *Below* South Moor Colliery Silver Prize Band, 1907. Colliery bands were an important feature of the social life in pit villages. This one is from South Moor, near Stanley in County Durham The band were participants in a contest at the Crystal Palace on 28 September, 1907, in which nearly 150 bands took part. The test piece was ''Gems of Schumann'', and the Grand Shield was won by South Moor

36 *Right* Miner's Eviction, 1891. This photograph, from the publisher's collection, shows the effects of the eviction of Mr G. Bousfield and his family. Having nowhere to go, the family is forced to make do in a lean-to at the end of a chapel building. It had long been the custom in the mining industry, when strikes were in force, for the coalowners to recruit new sources of labour from different parts of the country. When these new persons arrived, a home was needed, therefore the striking miners were evicted to make room for the newcomers

37 *Below right* Ashington Colliery. In 1896 Ashington was described as ''one of the latest marvels of the Northumberland coalfield''. The first shaft was sunk in 1846, but the Ashington Coal Company was not founded until 1866

SOUTH MOOR COLLIERY SILVER PRIZE BAND.
THE GRAND SHIELD AT CRYSTAL PALACE CONTEST ON SEP 28 1907

ASHINGTON COLLIERY. 1044. W.M.

AGRICULTURE

38 *Left* Blacksmith's Shop, Cullercoats, 1899. Mather's Blacksmith's shop was in back Huddleston Street, Cullercoats. The two workers are Mr William Younger and Mr Jack Bolam

39 *Right* Lanercost Smithy, close to the Northumberland border in Cumberland. Work is in progress on a plough

40 *Below* Near Mitford, *c*.1900. A happy lunchtime break in the fields. This photo shows the rough coarse aprons, often sacking, which were worn by the women to protect their clothing

41 Sheep shearing at Mitford in Northumberland, *c.*1900. The two shearers are on the right of the picture while the woman is gathering together the fleeces and working as hard as the men

42 *Above* Haymaking at Mitford about 1900. The woman's bonnet served a useful purpose in keeping the sun off the back of the neck while working

43 *Right* Dairy maids all-in-a-row, *c*.1896. Taken in County Durham, this photograph is from Lord Londonderry's collection. The barrel-shaped "end-over-end" type butter churns can be seen against the wall. The butter was made by turning it over and over, by way of a handle, with a steady rhythmic movement. The tables in the centre of the room are called butter-workers. These are wooden draining tables fitted with wooden rollers. They were used for consolidating the butter grains and for expelling moisture from butter

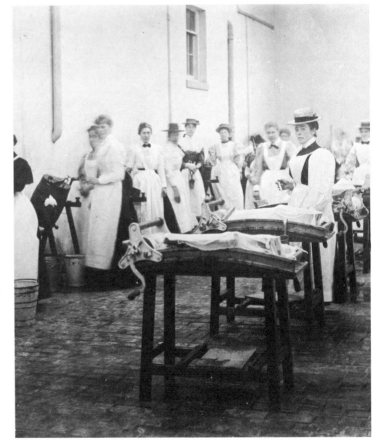

TEACHING

44 Jesmond Presbyterian Church Mission, *c.*1910. Liverpool Street Mission, in one of the worst slums in the town, was started a few years before the opening of Jesmond Presbyterian Church. In 1888 the Mission came under the charge of the Jesmond Church and remained with it to its closure, when Liverpool Street was demolished in 1927. The number of meetings at the Mission every week was considerable. The Mother's Meeting (seen in this photograph), on Wednesday afternoons, had a very warm-hearted membership, who enjoyed the social life of the meeting, and who found useful the Benefit Club, the Clothing Club, and the Savings Club

45 Wellesley Training Ship, *c.*1895. An interior view of the mess deck on this famous nineteenth-century Tyneside ship. The ship was used as a training vessel for destitute boys. Presented by the Admiralty, she arrived in the Tyne in June 1868. She was a 50-gun frigate, with accommodation for 250 to 300 boys. Any boy found begging, wandering, or destitute could be committed to the ship, where he would remain until he was 16 and be given the usual elementary education, plus shipboard duties

46 Mission House, Walbottle, *c.*1905: A group of children photographed outside the Mission House in Walbottle, a small village a few miles west of Newcastle, on the main road to Carlisle. This Mission Room was erected in 1892 by public subscription

47 *Right* Denton Road School, Newcastle, 1910. The sewing class at this council primary school in the West end suburb of Scotswood. The school was opened only a couple of years before the photograph was taken

48 *Below* Cambo School, *c*.1890. There are about 68 children in this class. The teacher was Ellen Richardson, but she did have an assistant, who is also seen in the photograph. The school was built, with a master's residence, in 1886 by Sir Charles Trevelyan, Bart, for 150 children, the average attendance being 65

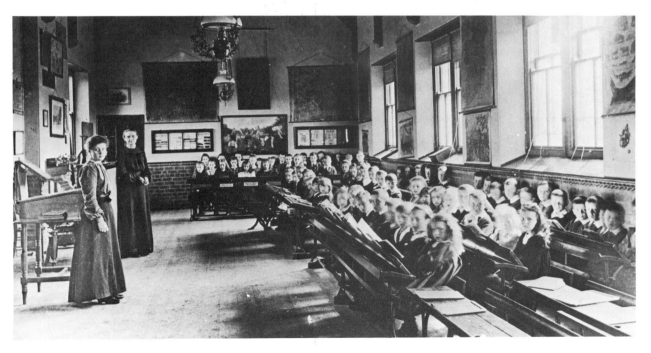

NEWCASTLE UPON TYNE

49 *Below* Percy Street, 1897: a famous old corner of Newcastle. Originally called Sidgate, the street was re-named in compliment to the ducal family of Northumberland. The cottages date from the mid-seventeenth century and were demolished *c.*1963

50 *Right* Blackett Street, one of the main City centre arteries, in 1903. The old Central Library can be seen in the background, and behind it, the construction works for the Laing Art Gallery Tower. The building was presented to the city by Mr Alexander Laing, a wealthy wine merchant, and was opened by Viscount Ridley in 1904. Tramcar No 92 can be seen making its way to Central Railway Station. This was a class 'F' car built by Newcastle Corporation Transport in 1903

51 *Below right* Sandgate, *c.*1897: one of the most ancient streets in Newcastle. As its name implies, the Sand Gate of the old walls was built on the sand at the side of the river at the end of the street. Sandgate was the home of the keelmen who worked on the coal-lighters and who were a race by themselves. It is world-famous because of the song ''The Keel Row'' which begins ''As I came thro' Sandgate''. The pump or pant which can be seen at the end of the street ran beer instead of water in honour of George IV's coronation (July 1821)

OLD HOUSES SANDGATE NEWCASTLE. 68.

52 High Level and Swing Bridges: The High Level Bridge (road with railway on top) was built by Robert Stephenson in 1849 to carry the rail traffic on the East Coast Route to Scotland. The Swing Bridge was one of the first large opening bridges of its kind. It was opened in 1876. The swinging property enabled large vessels to pass up and down river to and from the Elswick Works of the Armstrong Company. The paddle steamer on the left is the *Cowen*, built in 1859, and that on the right, built in 1864, is the *Mariner*

53 *Left* Newgate Street, Newcastle, in 1911. The Empire Palace Theatre is decorated in honour of the coronation of King George V. This Empire, one of the famous circuit of Moss Empires, was built in 1903 on the site of a previous Empire. It continued in business until the 1960s when it was demolished to make way for the Swallow Hotel and Newgate Shopping Precinct

54 *Below left* Newcastle Public Library, *c*.1895. The original Central Library, opened in 1881, was built on the site of the Carliol Tower, part of the medieval walls of Newcastle. The building was demolished in 1969 to make way for a new road, part of the A1 north to Edinburgh. In 1904 the Laing Art Gallery was built and the two buildings were at right-angles at that point. The Church of Divine Unity next to the Library was pulled down in the late 1930s. The other Church, Trinity Presbyterian, was demolished in the 1960s. The old Library was designed by A. M. Fowler. The left-hand portion was originally the Mechanics Institute and was built in 1866

55 *Below* Northumberland Road, *c*.1911: The Olympia was built in 1892 for the Olympia Theatre Company and was owned by them until 1899 when it was bought by Dick Thornton, of music-hall fame. After this it was leased to Ralph Pringle's North American Animated Picture Company to become Newcastle's first regular cinema. It was eventually demolished in 1971, having been closed in 1960. The adjoining building is the White City which was built at about the same time as the rebuilt Olympia

56 The Side, *c.*1893: a narrow, steep street leading from the Cathedral, the tower of which can be seen in the background, to Sandhill, and the Quayside. This was part of the Great North Road to Edinburgh in coaching days. Its unusual name comes from the fact that the street stands on the side of the hill on which the Castle was located

57 Grainger Street, 1897. The Grey Monument can be seen at the far end of the street. This was erected, by public subscription, to the memory of Earl Grey, of Great Reform Bill fame, in 1838. The column was designed by a local man, Benjamin Green. The street is named after Richard Grainger, who with the architect John Dobson was responsible for the design and rebuilding of the city centre in the 1830s. The lower section of the street, in the foreground, was constructed in the late 1860s, some 30 years after the top section

58 *Right* Brandling Village, c.1910: a small, more-or-less self-contained suburb within the township of Jesmond. During the course of the nineteenth century this township changed entirely from country fields into a dense suburb of Newcastle. In 1821 the land belonging to Robert Warwick was sold to Newcastle builders who erected the houses which form Brandling Village

59 *Below* Barras Bridge, c.1895. The church is that of St Thomas the Martyr. Designed by John Dobson, it was built between 1825 and 1830. The Grand Hotel, on the left of the picture, was built in 1890.

A BIT OF OLD NEWCASTLE. 5595. G.H. N/C.

60 *Left* Central Station and
Neville Street, *c*.1895. Both
hansom cabs and horse trams
can be seen in the picture. The
Central Station, designed by
John Dobson of Newcastle,
was built between 1846 and
1850. St Mary's Roman Catholic
Cathedral, seen in the background, is by Pugin, and was
built in 1844. The spire was
added between 1860 and 1873
to a design by Hansom. The
County Hotel, opposite the
Portico, was built in the 1870s
to 1880s to designs by M. H.
Graham

61 *Below left* St John's Lane,
c.1868, a very narrow, cobbled
street, part of old Newcastle
which was demolished in 1868
to make way for the extension
of Grainger Street from Bigg
Market down to the Central
Railway Station

62 *Below* Grainger Street,
Newcastle, 1911, decorated in
honour of the coronation of
King George V. All of the
buildings seen on this
photograph are still standing.
The tram is of the Class D type,
open top with reversed stairs,
built by the Brush Company in
1905

MARKETS AND SHOPS

63 *Below* London and Newcastle Tea Company, *c.*1900: the staff posing outside the Waterloo Road branch in Blyth. This company was founded in the 1870s

64 *Right* Green Market, Newcastle, 1908: the shop of Messrs Moody and Evans. Probably taken in the springtime of 1908; the daffodils and tulips appear to be at their best. Sadly, the Market is no more

65 *Below right* Fruit sellers outside the Portico of the Central Station, *c.*1898. In the background can be seen the two separate hotels, on the left the Victoria Hotel and on the right the Comet Hotel, later to become "The Victoria and Comet". Next door is one of the famous Lockhart Cocoa Rooms

66 Still a most popular venue for Tynesiders, the Sunday morning market on Newcastle Quayside has been held regularly since way back in the last century. It starts at about 10 o'clock and wanders on until 1 or 2 o'clock in the afternoon

67 Stewart's, Grainger Street, Newcastle, c.1896: a renowned Newcastle tea merchant. The opening between Stewart's and Isaac Walton's leads into the large covered market known as the Butcher or Grainger Market

68 Alnwick Market Place, c.1892. The Market Cross is in the foreground, and from here the great announcements of peace and war were proclaimed. On his several visits to Alnwick, John Wesley usually preached from the steps of the Cross. On the far side of the Square is the Town Hall, which was built by the freemen of Alnwick, whose ancient Corporation dates back to 1160

69 Paddy's Market, Newcastle, c.1895. This street is called Milk Market, although Milk is not sold there. What is sold is old clothes. The market still takes place today, and must be well over one hundred years old

70 Tilley's, Blackett Street, Newcastle, c.1908: one of the most famous and popular restaurants in Newcastle. The shop on the right belonged to T. & G. Allan, booksellers, until 1974 when it was taken over by John Menzies

71 Barnard Castle Market Place, *c.*1895. A very congested scene, but the layout enables the fine features of the buildings to be clearly seen. Most belong to the eighteenth or early nineteenth centuries

72 Grainger Market, Newcastle, *c.*1912. Built by Richard Grainger to the designs of John Dobson, this "Butcher Market" was opened in 1835 and was the commercial hub of their scheme for central Newcastle.

73 *Above* Stockton-on-Tees Market, *c.*1899. One of the oldest features of Stockton is the Open Market. The weekly Wednesday market (and also a Fair every year upon the Feast of St Thomas the Martyr, to continue for eight days) was granted to the town by Antony Bec, Bishop of Durham in 1310

74 *Right* Market Place, Middlesbrough, *c.* 1895. The old Town Hall, seen in the centre of the Square, was built in 1846 by W. L. Moffat of Doncaster. The Market itself had first opened on 12 December 1840. Behind the old Town Hall is the tower of St Hilda's Parish Church

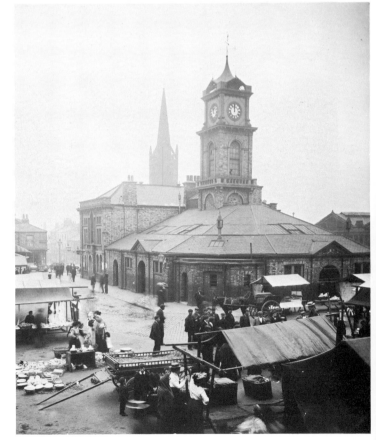

75 Market Place, South Shields, *c.*1896. The square building in the left centre is the old Town Hall, built in 1768. Opposite the Town Hall is St Hilda's Church, the tower of which also dates from 1768, and the rest of it from about 1810

76 Market Place, Morpeth, *c.*1900. The building on the left is the Town Hall, built in 1714 by Vanbrugh, but renewed in 1869–70 after fire damage, by Johnson. The tower on the right of the picture is the Town Steeple or Clock Tower which dates from the seventeenth century

77 Quayside Market, *c.*1910: the Sunday morning market on Newcastle Quayside; a general shot giving a better idea of how popular and crowded this regular feature of Tyneside life was (and still is)

AMUSEMENTS AND PASTIMES

78 On the Lion Bridge, Alnwick, c.1904

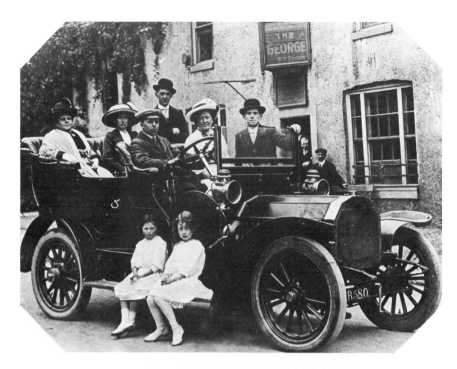

79 *Left* Piercebridge, Durham: outside the George Hotel, *c.*1908. (Is the car one of the early Dennis models? Certainly the shape of the radiator and bonnet is the same)

80 *Below* The Skating rink in Exhibition Hall, St Mary's Place, Newcastle, 1911. The Hall was erected in 1907, and a year later it was turned into a skating rink to meet the demands of the national roller skating craze. The skating craze lasted only a few years, and by 1914 the Hall reverted to its original purpose

SKATING RINK NEWCASTLE.

81 On the sands at Whitley Bay, *c.*1892

82 A performing bear in Bondgate, Darlington, *c.*1895

DURHAM IN WINTER. 5058. G.H.N/C.

83 Durham in Winter 1895. During later Victorian and Edwardian times, every opportunity which presented itself for ice-skating was swooped upon. Rivers and lakes were not available very often, but the populace of Durham were obviously enjoying this frosty spell when the River Wear was frozen during the very cold winter of 1894–95

84 In Tynemouth Park, 1895. The building on the left is the Plaza, a centre for indoor amusements, and behind this is the beach and the North Sea

85 Skating at Alnwick 1895. On the River Aln at Alnwick, Northumberland. The view shows the Lion Bridge, with the famous Percy Lion adorning the parapet. The winter of 1894–95 was one of those which have gone into the record books along with 1946–47 and 1962–63

86 A game of marbles in Elswick Park, in the western suburbs of Newcastle, *c.*1895

87 Wil Hunter's Tynemouth Pierrots, 1907

WIL HUNTER'S TYNEMOUTH PIERROTS. 1907.

88 Exchange Walk, Newcastle, on 14 May 1904. The 1904 race was the second annual event promoted by the Newcastle Commercial Exchange. There were 104 entries, although only 78 started the $40\frac{1}{2}$ mile walk between Newcastle boundary and Haltwhistle. Mr T. S. M. Carbarns was the winner with a time of seven hours 34 minutes. The first prize was £5

89 The Mitford Band, or orchestra, formed by Miss B. K. MacLeod, the Vicar of Mitford's daughter. She is seated in the centre of the front row with her baton and her father, the Vicar, is on the left-hand side of the back row. The date is June 1909

90 Bamburgh Golf Course, *c.*1910. Opened in 1904, it was an 18-hole course with a good clubhouse which can be seen on the left. A guide book of the period states 'This is also a Workmen's Golf Club by which the Artisan class can enjoy "the royal and ancient game" by paying a small nominal fee'

91 Tynedale Foxhounds in the grounds of Swinburne Castle. The Master at the time of this photograph was Mr John Coppin Straker, who held the position for over half a century from 1883 to 1937

92 During the 1898 provincial tour of Barnum and Bailey's "Greatest Show on Earth", the circus visited Newcastle. This picture shows the zebras being off-loaded at Forth Goods Station

93 On Whitley Bay Sands, *c.*1900

94 At the seaside, 1909. The children are members of the Spring Blossom Juvenile Temple, the junior section of one of the Newcastle lodges of the Independent Order of Good Templars. This picture was taken at Whitley Bay

95 At High Cross House in Benwell, now a suburb at the west end of Newcastle, 1900. The house stood at the top of what is now St John's Road. The gentleman in the bowler hat was Thomas King, a leading figure in the Band of Hope, and the girls in the picture are from that organisation

96 A visit to Warkworth, 1908, by one of the Newcastle lodges of the Independent Order of Good Templars. Note the box camera being held by the young man in the front row. In the background are the ruins of Warkworth Castle

NORTHUMBERLAND

97 This was one of the main shopping streets in Blyth (*c.*1892), which attracted shoppers from the whole of the Blyth valley area of South-East Northumberland

98a and b Indoor staff and stable staff, at Doxford Hall, near Ellingham, *c.*1894. The hall was built by John Dobson in 1818. At one time it belonged to the family of Major A. S. C. Browne of Callaly Castle

99 Situated at the north end of Turner Street, Blyth, was this typically Victorian example of railway architecture (*c.*1902). It was originally the property of a private company, The Blyth and Tyne Railway

100 Table Rocks, Whitley Bay, *c.*1910. The radio mast belongs to the Cullercoats Wireless Station, one of the first in England, built in 1908

101 Bridge Street, Morpeth, *c.*1898. In the early part of the nineteenth century, Bridge Street, along with the neighbouring Newgate Street and Market Place, was the scene of the weekly market for fat cattle and sheep which was the great feature of life in Morpeth in those days. By the time this photograph was taken, the weekly market was held only in Market Place

102 One of the three beaches at Tynemouth, this is known locally as the Long Sands (*c.*1895)

103 Tynemouth Priory, *c.*1895: a parade of members of the Royal Artillery (Volunteers) who were garrisoned at Tynemouth Castle. The lighthouse, which can be seen to the left of the picture, was built about 1775 on the site of an earlier one and was demolished in 1898

104 Main Street, Warkworth, from the Castle looking down towards the Parish Church of St Lawrence in the distance (c.1900)

105 Amble Harbour, *c.*1895. There were 5 staithes from which the coal could be shipped. Some of these can be seen in the picture

AMBLE HARBOUR. 356

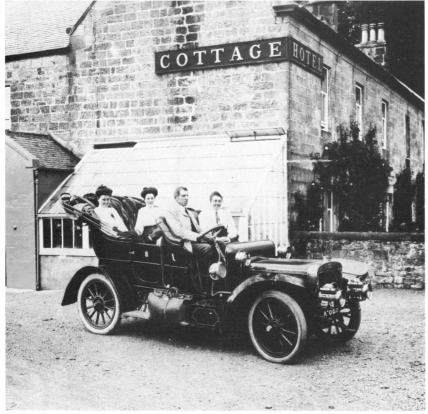

106 *Above* Looking down the main street, Bamburgh, with the Castle in the distance

107 *Left* At the Cottage Hotel, Wooler, *c.*1907. This is still in existence, but is now called the Tankerville Arms. The registration number of the car begins with the letter ''X'', which was Northumberland's original registration letter and commenced in 1904

108 Children playing round the famous Percy Lion, with Alnwick Castle in the background, *c*.1890

EVENTS AND OCCASIONS

109 Unveiling the Victoria Monument, Newcastle, 1903. The ceremony was performed by the Countess Grey on 24 April. The statue was designed in bronze by A. Gilbert and was erected in St Nicholas Square in commemoration of the 500th anniversary of the Shrievalty of Newcastle

110a and b Two views of the Northumberland Agricultural show, held at Morpeth in 1895. One picture shows the inside of the butter tent where all the processes and implements of butter making are being exhibited

111 *Turbinia*: the first vessel to be driven by a steam turbine (1897). This was the achievement of Sir Charles Parsons, Tyneside-born engineer who eventually gained international recognition for his invention of the steam turbine. He began work on his invention in a little wooden hut on the banks of the Tyne at Wallsend in 1894. What eventually emerged from that hut was *Turbinia*, some 90 feet long and weighing 44 tons. In the early trials, she achieved a speed of 28 knots. *Turbinia* is now housed in the Museum of Science and Engineering at Newcastle

112 Shipwreck at Whitley Bay, 1898. The *Luna* was a Danish ship, registered at Svendborg. A wooden schooner of 123 tons, she was built by C. J. Jensen of Troense in 1858 for P. Jensen and Company

113 *Left* Members of the
Northumberland Hussars and
Durham County Contingent of
the Imperial Yeomanry marching
down Bath Lane in Newcastle
on their return home from the
Boër War, 1903

114 *Below left* A fine variety of
horse-drawn vehicles arriving
(*c*.1908) at Wynyard Park, the
seat of the Marquis of
Londonderry, near Stockton-
on-Tees in County Durham, for
an afternoon excursion

115 *Below* The lifeboat is being
launched (*c*.1870) at Tynemouth
to go to the assistance of a
vessel in difficulties off the
Black Middens

116 *Left* A parade of a group of non-militant suffragettes, 1912, in Northumberland Street, Newcastle, advertising *The Common Cause*, the news-sheet of the National Union of Women's Suffrage Societies

117 *Below left* Baalfire at Whalton: a photograph taken on St John's Eve, 4 July 1903. This was an annual custom. As the sun went down on 4 July a huge bonfire was made and lit on the village green at Whalton, near Morpeth in Northumberland. As the fire burned up, a fiddle or some other instrument was procured, and the young people began to dance around the fire. The origin of the custom is probably very ancient. The photograph is probably by Sir Benjamin Stone, MP, who, in 1903, was invited to Whalton

118 *Below* King Edward VII and Queen Alexandra leaving Newcastle Central Railway Station on 11 July 1906. The purpose of the visit to Newcastle was threefold: the opening of the Armstrong College (now part of the University of Newcastle); the opening of the Royal Victoria Infirmary; and the unveiling of the statue of Queen Victoria in front of the Infirmary

119 The aftermath of a great fire in October 1854 on Newcastle quayside. In the early morning of the 6th a fire was discovered in a worsted factory in Gateshead, which in less than an hour entirely gutted the building. Next to it was a warehouse containing sulphur and nitrate of soda. This also caught fire and just after three o'clock in the morning there was an almighty explosion which hurled burning missiles over the river, and set alight houses on the Newcastle quay

120 This memorial in Bishopwearmouth Cemetery, Sunderland, depicts a mother holding her dead child, and commemorates a sad incident which took place in June 1883, only eleven years after the Victoria Hall, a provincial version of the Albert Hall, was opened. The tragedy occurred when 183 children were suffocated and crushed in a stampede, rushing down the stairs to secure a distribution of free toys at the end of a special children's entertainment

121 Albert Edward Docks, North Shields, 1884: The last great work of the Tyne Commission before the completion of the Piers was the construction of the Coble Dene or Albert Edward Dock. Construction work began in 1873, and after several disruptions was completed in 1884. The picture is of the opening on 20 August of that year by their Royal Highnesses the Prince and Princess of Wales

122 A ceremonial arch set up at the seaward end of Front Street, Tynemouth in honour of the visit (1884) of the Prince and Princess of Wales to open the Albert Edward Dock at North Shields

123 The harbour of the fishing
village of Cullercoats on Regatta
Day in 1887. The building on
the beach, to the left of the
picture, is the Salt Water Bath,
which was erected in 1807

TRANSPORT

124 North Shields Ferry, *c*.1900: a steam-paddle ferry, known locally as the ''Penny Ferry'' operating between North and South Shields, on either banks of the River Tyne

125 Horse buses parked at the Newcastle end of the High Level Bridge (c.1900). The keep of the Castle can be seen behind the railway bridge. These buses, which carried 26 passengers, ferried people over the High Level Bridge between Newcastle and Gateshead at a fare of one halfpenny. The service began in the 1880s and continued until 1931, even after the electric trams started operating over the bridge in 1923

126 Newcastle Central Station, c.1904: platform 8, one of the main line platforms where trains from London to Edinburgh stop. To the left is the clock, under which people always arranged (and still do) to meet. The Central Station was designed by Newcastle architect John Dobson and cost £100,000. Work began in 1847 and the station was opened in August 1850 by Queen Victoria. Engine number 1868 standing at platform 8 is a Worsdell NER Class 0. 110 of this type were built between 1894 and 1901 with Stephenson valve gear. The last one was not withdrawn until 1958

127 Level Crossing, New Shildon. Work is in progress to widen the level crossing at Shildon in County Durham. Shildon figures prominently in railway history. The Stockton and Darlington Railway Company had workshops here and in 1827 it was decided to construct an engine in these shops. The result was the famous ''Royal George'' which started work on 29 November 1827

128 St John's Chapel, *c*.1890, with the horse-drawn stage used for ferrying passengers between St John's Chapel and Stanhope in Co Durham. The building outside which the coach is standing is The King's Arms hotel and posting house. The coach ran twice daily at 7 am and 3.20 pm

129 Lumley Ferry on the River Wear near Chester-le-Street, *c*.1890. The ferryman in 1890 was one William Curry

130 Rowlands Gill station (*c*.1900) on the Derwent Valley Line opened for passenger traffic on 2 December 1867. The line finally closed in 1954, Rowlands Gill being the last station left open

131 Blyth Ferry (*c*.1900): a chain-operated wooden steam ferry which began operations in 1889. It continued in service until 1965

132 Mr J. R. Ellerby and colleague, who were employed by the Cleveland Car Company of Grange Road, Darlington, which commenced trading about 1907–8. The car on the left is very similar in design to a 1908 Cadillac

133a and b Tynemouth Station, *c*.1902. Tynemouth was originally the end of the Newcastle to Tynemouth Railway, the line having been completed in 1864. (The line had ended at North Shields until then.) The new station, pictured here, was opened on 3 July 1882, when a new section of track linking Tynemouth with Monkseaton was inaugurated

134 Hartlepool Ferry, 1890. This photograph is taken from Middleton looking towards Town Wall and Victoria Dock. The toll was one halfpenny each way

135 A single-deck horse tram (1901) resting on Westgate Road, outside the old workhouse (now the General Hospital). The trams operated from Bentinck Road to Grey's Monument in the City Centre

136 Laying of tram-lines, 1901, at the top of Grainger Street in Newcastle round Grey's Monument, ready for electrification. The first electric trams commenced operations on 16 December 1901, by which date nearly 15 miles of track were ready for use

ISLANDS

137 *Below* Crossing from Holy Island at low tide by the old Pilgrim Way, *c.*1907. The box-like structure is a refuge in case anyone was caught by the tide when crossing

138 *Right* Farne Islands, *c.*1907. A coble is lying at the west door of the Longstone lighthouse, once the home of Grace Darling. It was from here in 1838 that she performed her heroic deed. The lighthouse's exterior remains virtually unchanged since her day

139 *Below right* Post carts at Holy Island, *c.*1907. Mr Robert Bell was postmaster, proprietor of a conveyance business and grocer on the island

140 St Mary's (or Bate's Island, as it was formerly known) lies off the Northumberland coast at Whitley Bay. This photograph (c.1892) shows the island before the erection of its famous lighthouse landmark. The building, partly tiled and partly thatched, was built in 1855 by a Scottish fisherman called George Ewen. The lighthouse was built on the Island in 1896–7

141 Farne Islands, *c*.1904. Rev. R. C. MacLeod, Vicar of Mitford, embarking at the Farne Islands after a photographic expedition. This photograph shows well how a Northumbrian coble could be brought into shallow water and beached stern first

142 Farne Islands, *c*.1910. A sailing coble lying at Staple Island, which is cut off at high tide from Brownsman Island opposite. The tall rectangular building is the remains of an early lighthouse or beacon where, on the top, coal fires were burnt nightly. The cottage was once the home of Grace Darling

PEOPLE

143 Mr E. L. Osbaldeston Mitford, FRGS, celebrated his 100th birthday on 31 October 1911. Celebrations were carried on for a number of days and one of these events was the Meet held on 2 November. The photograph shows (the back) Mr Osbaldeston Mitford and beside him his second wife whom he married in 1896

144 The marriage of Mr Bertram Lane Mitford of Mitford Castle and Miss Brenda Katherine MacLeod, elder daughter of the Rev. R. C. MacLeod, Vicar of Mitford and Mrs MacLeod on 11 August 1909

145 Abel Chapman, the Northumbrian naturalist and author, in his study. Born in Sunderland in 1815, Abel Chapman's fame came from his books about wild life and his collection of birds' eggs, stuffed birds and big game trophies

146 An afternoon tea party at the home of Lord Londonderry at Wynyard Park, Co Durham, *c*.1900

147 Cycling Party at Bothal (1902) at the entrance of Bothal Haugh, home of the Hon. and Rev. William Charles Ellis, MA, JP, rector of Bothal

148 Northumberland Street, Newcastle, 1898. An old hawker, seen in what is now one of
Newcastle's busiest thoroughfares, formerly part of the Great North Road

149 Thomas Burt speaking at the Northumberland Miners Gala at Tynemouth, *c*.1910. Mr Burt progressed from pit-boy to privy councillor during a period when such rises were much less common than they are today